Practical Keys to Raise the Dead

Written by Michael King

This book and other titles by Michael King can be found at TheKingsofEden.com and on Amazon.com

ISBN-13: 978-1-946252-00-5
Printed in the USA

Table of Contents

Dedication

I dedicate this book to all the resurrectionists out there—those men and women of faith who stand firm on the fact that Jesus is alive and His resurrection power is great enough to bring life out of death.

Preface

What do you do when you are standing in front of a dead body—scream and wail as you fall apart, stare quietly in sadness, or bring him back to life? If you are anything like me, you believe that Jesus is the only real hope we have in this world, so you will do your best to be faithful to the hope He has given us— that even if we die, we shall live (John 11:25).

This book isn't about theology, but instead will help you figure out what to do when you are standing in front of a body in need of resurrection. How do you pray? How long should you pray? How can you be prepared for if and when he awakes? What if he were an organ donor or were cremated—can he still be raised? This book will answer these questions and more.

This book will challenge long-held beliefs, and has the potential to offend as you read. If you can keep your heart and mind open, I believe that you will discover and learn Practical Keys to Raise the Dead.

CHAPTER 1

RIGHT AFTER DEATH

When someone dies in the United States, especially if he is in a hospital, a clock starts ticking. First, unless a Do Not Resuscitate (DNR) order is in place, medical personnel will activate what is known as the "chain of life" and attempt to resuscitate, but if that fails, then another string of events begins. In most states there is a 24-hour time window from the moment he dies to the time the body needs to be picked up by a mortician. A funeral director or his associates will usually deliver the body to a funeral home for embalming—a process that replaces the blood of the deceased with chemicals to prevent the body from decaying. While embalming is wonderful for anyone who wants to have an open-casket viewing a week later, it is comparatively less fantastic for those of us who want to raise the dead. The best thing to do when someone dies is immediately pray and command life into his body—for a few reasons.

- At the moment of death, every cell in the body begins to break down. The less time passes, the less repair the body will require to sustain life again.

- The body still has blood in the bloodstream instead of toxic preservatives in its place.

- From a faith-perspective, praying close to the time of death will usually feel easier than it will four days later, regardless of whether it actually is easier or not.

- The spirit is usually still right there in the room—it can even take up to a few hours in some cases for the spirit of the deceased to even realize that the body died and for him or her to begin whatever spiritual journey he or she will undertake. If you can get the spirit back in the body while it's still right there in the room, so much the better. (While this point may be questionable to some, a common theme observed in many near-death experiences is that one does not always instantly go "elsewhere" on death.)

If you are a family member present at the hospital, simply ask the hospital staff to leave you alone with your loved one—you can do this for *hours* if you just let them know you need "time to say goodbye." Don't bother telling them what you are doing—while there is a slim chance they would pray with you (I'm a nurse and would be glad to join in if it were my patient), more likely they won't be and will think you are nuts—and that won't help. Unless you have already formed a relationship with a staff member and know he or she is on board, just shut the door and do your thing. The nurses can put a sign on the door informing any staff or visitors to see the nurse (and thus leave you alone) before entering the room. It is not uncommon for staff to let a family have a hospital room for possibly up to half a day if the hospital isn't busy and demand for the room to put a living patient in is low. Keep in mind the nurse will probably want to come in and wash the body (it often defecates at death), raise the head of the bed to prevent blood from pooling in the face, and one or two other preparatory things. These are not required but nurses tend to do them as a courtesy, and if they ask to perform those tasks, they aren't being rude or anti-resurrection—they are simply trying to care for the body in the way they know how, and it can influence how the face appears if there is a viewing. With that said, staff also understand that each family has its own grieving process, possibly even cultural or religious rituals to perform at time of death, and that visitors will often travel even hours after death to say goodbye. Use that to your advantage—just don't be loud. The louder you are and the more ruckus you make, the more resistance and interruptions you will get from staff. Plus, louder prayers do not increase the likelihood of resurrection.

If you are somewhere other than a hospital or nursing home, you will probably be calling emergency medical services for help. If you can, do CPR. Under *no circumstances* should CPR be avoided or ignored in some vain attempt to prove that God's power is greater. God is all about life in every way—if you can do chest compressions, pray while doing them if it doesn't mess up your counting. If CPR fails, you can always fall back on praying for resurrection as the only intervention, but CPR is effective and is worth doing. Use human wisdom as well as Godly power for best results. In the end, if CPR is what brings them back, they're alive and you have accomplished your goal.

If the individual clearly died long before you arrived and CPR won't help, you might as well take a few minutes to pray for him before calling the police, ambulance, or coroner to notify them. Truthfully, once the authorities arrive, the body will go away and if the death is unexpected, an autopsy will usually be performed. Even if you are the spouse or parent, you may not get a choice in the matter. The body can't get more dead than it already is, so a short delay won't hurt. On the other hand, I don't recommend waiting for hours to notify the authorities. If there truly was foul play, it would make you look awfully suspicious and could impede a murder investigation—neither of which is good. If nothing happens in a short time after praying, go ahead and make the call.

Depending on which state the death occurred in and the length of time the deceased will remain unburied, you *may not be required* to embalm the body. However, if the individual died out of state and is being transported, the laws of one of the states involved may require it. One problem you may run into is that in order to *avoid* embalming, you may also have to bury the deceased within 24 hours. This is an unfortunate and extremely prohibitive timeline when it comes to resurrection, but God is bigger than chemicals, so even if it has to occur, it isn't going to stop a miracle. Keep in mind that it is uncommon *not* to embalm unless cremating, so you may get some push-back depending on the professionals involved.

Settling the issue of embalming is one of those times where knowing state laws on the subject comes in handy. Unfortunately, right when someone dies isn't usually the most opportune time to start doing research about your legal rights regarding death and burial. Equally problematic is the fact that there are 50 states in the USA and all of them have different rules—so there's no guaranteed easy way to know what is legal in your state. In spite of this fact, there are some online references that can help with this task. Search "burial laws by state" in a search engine and/or "burial laws in ____" and put in your state's name. The first two or three pages should yield useful results.

To help you along, I have found a few places you can contact that may help you sort out your legal rights regarding embalming, home burial, and more. The resources listed below do not have anything to do with resurrection—they are funeral-related organizations. These are mostly non-mainstream groups due to their focus on green burials (without embalming, etc.), home burials (with no funeral home involvement), etc. and as such think outside the box more than usual.

National Home Funeral Alliance (NHFA)
    http://homefuneralalliance.org/the-law/
Funeral Consumers Alliance
    https://www.funerals.org/consumers/legalyour-rights/
Green Burial Council
    http://greenburialcouncil.org/
Burial Legal Reference Online
    http://www.nolo.com/legal-encyclopedia/burial-cremation-laws

Remember, time is not on your side. You must move quickly and decisively, and the longer you take to make decisions, the more decisions will be made for you. If you plan to have the body at home, to not embalm, etc. you must make arrangements and proceed quickly. If not, the body will travel through the appropriate channels until you have access again at the funeral home after embalming. Preferably, if death is imminent, while continuing to pray for healing, it is best to review the above resources and make plans proactively so that time is on your side if and/or when the individual passes away.

Chapter 2

The Body Has Been Taken—Now What?

If you opted (or were forced) to embalm and/or are going the funeral-home route, you will have to wait for a few hours—the time it takes to embalm the body. What do you do while you wait? Go home. Sleep. Eat. Shower. When I say "Wait" I don't mean "Do nothing." In this short time until you get access to the body again, you can be praying up a storm or raising up an army of faith-filled people to support you. You might consider contacting your local church if you have one as the church may be able to help you with some aspects of the resurrection and may be willing to join you in prayer. Consider activating a prayer chain if the organization has one. Put a post on social media. Google the Resurrection Prayer Map and connect with someone nearby to come join you physically in prayer. Contact the Raise the Dead Initiative and Dead Raising Team via website or social media to join in prayer as well. Their contact information is as follows:

Raise the Dead Initiative:

http://www.thekingsofeden.com/raise-the-dead-initiative/

https://www.facebook.com/groups/124203581018584/

Dead Raising Team:

http://www.deadraisingteam.com/

https://www.facebook.com/groups/57430291805/

The one caveat I will give at this point is that more is not necessarily better. When Jesus went to raise Jairus' daughter, he kicked some people out of the room. The more people who know you are going for resurrection, the more naysayers, skeptics, and doubters you will alert, and let me tell you—the enemy will mobilize them in full force. This does not necessarily mean you should be secretive or keep it from your church, family, and friends, nor does it mean you should shy away from posting on social media. What it *does* mean is that you want to use prayerful wisdom and discernment when you select your resurrection team. Many followers of Jesus are what I would call "unbelieving believers" and while they might be your closest friends, there is a good chance they're not going to help the cause. Try to differentiate between good friends and faith-filled friends, and if you find both in the same people, you are blessed!

Either before or after activating your personal intercessory team, contact the mortician to get an idea of when they will be finished. Explain that you are going to attempt to resurrect him. This is important for the funeral home to understand because they need to know you want access to the body as often as possible. You will need to set this up, which can be done either at the funeral home at agreed-upon times or at your church. If your church can house the body, it can stay there for a very long time— possibly weeks or longer if all parties are in agreement. Depending on state laws you may also be able to keep the body in your home. As mentioned before, the laws regarding storage and disposition of the body vary. The funeral home should be aware of these laws and be able to inform you of what is and is not possible. Nevertheless, you might still try to research these laws yourself just in case the funeral home gives you the run-around and thinks you are nuts. On the other hand, remember that this is the mortician's industry—dead bodies and grieving families are what they deal with on a daily basis. They probably have seen every imaginable reaction to death you can think of, and a few you can't. They may be sympathetic to your cause as has happened to other believers in the past. One woman I know had immense favor with the funeral home as the mortician was a follower of Jesus and believed in raising the dead. You never know what you will be up against, so prepare for the worst and pray for the best.

If the body is kept at the funeral home, you will have to set up hours of access with them for viewings and such, and usually you will have to rent the room space at a daily rate. This can get expensive but the business will most likely keep the body there as long as you are willing to pay. The church may or may not charge you anything for storage, and if it is your home church, you may be able to get a key to the building and permission to use the sanctuary or other designated location for praying over the body, whether at specific times or 24/7. This will vary from church to church based on the discretion of the church leadership. If you own your own home or property and keep the body there, you have a lot more leeway in that you can make the rules regarding access and time for prayer, again depending on state laws.

Chapter 3

Praying Over The Body

The ministries I have heard of worldwide who have significant success with resurrection have discovered one thing: It is preferable to spend hours and hours, possibly days on end praying over the body until the person resurrects. For whatever reason, when 24/7 intercession occurs on site, the resurrection seems to become more likely to a certain degree. This does not mean that it cannot happen under other circumstances, but that "best practice" is to have people pray continuously in shifts with the body until the individual returns to life or until the burial. If that is not possible, then anything is better than nothing. A simple "Live in Jesus' name" may be all it takes, and it could theoretically be done from a million miles away. Whether it is that proximity releases faith or whatever other reason I cannot say, but while it isn't required, it does seem to help. Thus, if you have the time and ability and preferably the help of others, pray around the clock in the presence of the body. This can go on for days, weeks, or months as God does not set a limit on when someone can be raised. I know a woman who seriously went after resurrection for two months before burying her husband, and I have heard stories of saints who resurrected decades-old bodies. With that in mind, time is not necessarily a limitation but it is best to make wise use of it nonetheless.

If you can, lay hands on the body. As mentioned before, physical proximity is not required, but I suggest that more people are raised from someone praying over them than someone praying from a million miles away—even though both can work.

Prayer is more than simply repeating words over and over. After about ten to twenty minutes you will have prayed through every scripture verse on resurrection and said every unique prayer you can think of. If it were about saying the right things, this would be a one-page book with the formula prayer and nothing else. It's not about reciting a formula but about releasing faith. Once you run out of things to pray, consider taking a break to stretch your legs or worship for a while. Come back and simply intend in your heart for the deceased person to return. Thank God for His goodness. Pray a little more. Worship some. Remind yourself of God's will to raise the dead, either silently or aloud. Soak in God's presence and/or engage in contemplative prayer about resurrection. Go to the bathroom, get a drink, but above all else, persist in ongoing prayer, and be as repetitive as you need so long as you recognize there is no formula.

Fasting is a good plan—there may not be a better time to fast than when attempting resurrection, but there may also not be a worse time. When fasting, people usually get tired more easily due to lack of an easily available energy source. You will likely be more sleepy, fatigue more easily, and may even get dizzy when standing up too quickly. These are all normal, but will all influence how your prayer-time goes. I'm not saying to avoid fasting, but if it's your first time, be aware that your blood sugar may drop and you will get tired, irritable, and may feel weak. Juice fasting is easier on the body than water-only fasts as you can still consume some sugars to help alleviate these symptoms. People tend to get cold more easily, so wear a jacket or have one available. On the other hand, you may feel more spiritually alive and clear-headed when not tired, and fasting has other spiritual benefits not covered here, so it can be a wise choice.

Just because someone does something in the Bible, doesn't make it a good idea for you here and now. If the funeral director (or a family member) sees you lying on top of the body because Elijah did it (2 Kings 4:32-35), you will probably be kicked out and could possibly be arrested depending on state laws. If this method fails, you may also have insulted every single family member present and they might never speak to you again. You had better be darn sure you heard from God before you use that particular "method" for resurrection, and for the record, it is not one I recommend.

Don't be afraid to address the demonic realms. Demons are directly involved each and every time a death occurs, and I have read many death-experiences where the deceased saw demons trying to prevent them from resurrection. This is a very real spiritual battle we wage to raise the dead, and demons actively try to oppose us. Bind them, command angels to destroy them and break their power; even consider breaking curses over the dead individual. Sometimes a person will die because of these types of spiritual problems. You might sense a need to do identificational repentance—where you apply God's forgiveness over the problem through prayer as though it were your problem. In this practice you are acting as a stand-in and pray as a representative in heaven on his behalf.

You may feel led to break generational curses, witchcraft, and may even feel the Lord leading you to do specific prophetic actions for this to occur. Keep in mind that while you may be hearing God, this can be a tricky situation. Part of me says, "Obey God wholeheartedly," but the other part of me recognizes that we are fallible and can hear incorrectly as well. If the prophetic act involves vandalism or destruction of facility property, that is a bad idea. If it involves the personal property of the deceased or a very disruptive action, you should probably ask permission from the appropriate party (if it isn't you) before proceeding. This is also a good time to test the idea out with other believers to see if everyone is in agreement that you are hearing from God. It's not a matter of majority-voting, but group discernment in accordance with the principle laid out in 1 Corinthians 14:29.

Don't be afraid to ask people *not* to be there. As stated before, more is not better. This isn't a heavenly popularity contest and God isn't keeping track of which people get more "likes" on social media to decide whether or not to raise the dead. Faith is key—if someone is filled with doubt and prays prayers like, "God, if it be your will to bring so-and-so back then let him return, but if it not be your will then keep him in heaven," I highly recommend you kick that person out, albeit politely. That approach isn't what you want around, and it has the potential to poison the faith of everyone else present. That

23

individual is just as likely to hurt the attempt as help it, and he or she clearly does not believe God wants to raise the deceased. Go where the faith is, even if that means you are the only person there.

Along similar lines, figure out those who are for you and those who are against you. As mentioned in a previous section, not everyone will applaud your faith-stance. Some will go so far as to actively oppose you. Recognize it for what it is—an attack of the enemy sent to destroy your faith and keep the individual dead. These oppositional individuals may be well-meaning but it doesn't change the fact that in that moment, they have become the voice of the enemy. I don't recommend treating them like the enemy because we war against the spirit, not against flesh and blood (Ephesians 6:12), but you will need to make firm boundaries with some people and ultimately shut them out of the effort if need be.

If you are leading the resurrection attempt, people really should respect your wishes during the period of prayer, especially if you are the spouse or other family member. If people cannot give you that respect, they do not need to be there. They do not have to agree with your decisions, regardless of what those decisions may be, but as long as it is legal, within reason, and related to the resurrection, they really should respect your choices anyway. Likewise, if you are not leading the attempt, you need to show the person(s) in charge the respect you would want if it were you. This isn't about being "in control" or about manipulation, but simple respect and decency, and honoring one another goes a long way in this sort of situation.

Put yourself in their shoes—they have lost their loved one and are getting bombarded from all sides. Don't increase the stress level any further—you are to be the solution, not the problem. If you feel the person leading the attempt *is* the problem, then it might simply not be the right time or place for you to be involved. When someone dies, it's not about a power trip, exerting control, or anything else—it is about bringing the dead back to life by the power of Jesus Christ. If you sense the Lord showing you that the person(s) in charge are holding up the resurrection, then pray accordingly, that God would open their eyes and even open a door for you to provide suggestions and/or solutions that will help. God is not limited and He can bring the right person at the right time to turn things around. Instead of getting frustrated and angry, which is the enemy's goal, turn that concern into intercession so that God's will is made more fully manifest. Turn the problems you discern into prayer requests to destroy powers of darkness that seek to hinder the attempt.

Be spirit-led, kind, and supportive. Give extra grace to everyone involved as tension can be high and the enemy wants to exploit any and every available access point. Don't be the one giving them the foothold they need.

Chapter 4

Physical
Considerations

While not necessarily the first things people think of
when attempting a resurrection, there are practical
actions you can take to make the entire unpleasant
process of dealing with a dead body a little more
amenable. When a resurrection attempt is successful,
some of these actions will also help things go more
smoothly after the fact.

- Keep the room temperature low, preferably
  60 degrees or lower because bodies decay
  more slowly in cooler temperatures. This is
  even more important if the body isn't
  embalmed and it might keep the smell down
  slightly longer. If prayer continues for weeks,
  the effect on the person's appearance will be
  significant. While not necessarily impacting
  the resurrection attempt, an air-conditioned
  body is more pleasing to the eye and may be
  more comforting to those present.

- Ancient cultures used myrrh and other highly aromatic spices after death for a reason. Essential oils may be used as a perfume to help cover the smell of decay, but you may need several bottles. An essential oil diffuser could help with this.

- Every single body is eligible for resurrection even if embalmed, cremated, burned, organs removed, missing limbs, etc. God is a creator and will make everything new. It's not based on percentage of body present but on the power of God. Don't let missing parts turn you away from your goal.

- Bring a change of clothes with you—for the deceased. Funeral homes cut the clothing down the back to dress the body easily, so clothing is usually like an apron—only covering the front and sides. When he or she awakes, it will get a bit windy back there and probably be rather embarrassing. Yes, at that point he or she is no longer dead so a little embarrassment isn't a big deal in comparison, but if you're going to go for it, you might as well come prepared with at least a robe. More preferable is a full change of clothes: shoes and socks, underwear, bra for the women, pants/dress, shirt, and sweatshirt or coat if the weather calls for it. I can't imagine being dead and then waking up only to be absolutely freezing—that sounds pretty unpleasant.

- If the body is at a church or person's house and you are going to be there for days without leaving, you might consider bringing a toothbrush, change of clothes, deodorant, etc. for yourself as well.

- Bring food and water to have on hand for the newly-resurrected person. From the stories I have heard, and even from Jesus' example in scripture (Mark 5:43), it is appropriate to give the person food and water upon his return, and he will often ask for it. Having it on hand not only makes things much easier, but it is an act of faith. If you think about it, having food (and clothes) on hand are what someone who is expecting results is going to do. Engaging in simple acts of faith that the person will be raised can help. Consider neatly placing the food and clothing near the casket, if one is used, as a visual reminder of the end-goal. Go expecting success and keep in mind that faith looks like something—then go and do whatever that looks like.

- If your spouse died and you have children, they will need a lot of love during this process. You may need to take a few hours away from praying to tend to their hurting hearts. This isn't a lack of faith on your part, even if it feels like it. It's loving your family through a really, *really* difficult time. And no one is going to pretend that it is easy—you are hurting as well and trying to stand in faith. It's a battle—but children don't always understand that, and they need what they need. Work to balance their needs with the ways the enemy may try to use them to drag you away from the resurrection. You have to be spirit-led on this—there is no easy answer.

CHAPTER 5

WHEN DO I QUIT PRAYING?

The whole stopping praying thing is difficult to communicate clearly in writing because it is so situational. It is hard to know when (or if) to stop actively pursuing resurrection, and the "when" will vary for each situation. Part of what makes the idea of ceasing a prayer attempt difficult is that the God of the Bible is the God of the living and it is *always* His will for everyone to be raised, every time, period. As such, there is never technically a "right time" to stop from a theological standpoint, but there may be one practically. The best I can do is give you some guidelines and ask questions that should help you to make the wisest decision possible for your circumstances.

Do you have the time to keep going? If you stop other things in your life, how long can you keep that up until it causes problems that will be hard to recover from whether the attempt fails or succeeds? For example, this may involve taking time off work.

If the attempt fails and you keep taking time off work such that you lose your job, you may be in far more hot water than just losing your loved one. On the other hand, if losing your job is what it takes to get your loved one back, it may well be worth it. If it were my wife or grandchild and all I had to do was give up my job to get them back, it would be an easy decision to make—but there are no guarantees. You may be able to use provisions under the Family Medical Leave Act (FMLA) to take unpaid time off during this period while keeping your job legally protected on your behalf. Talk to wise counsel and get advice on the best way to approach this issue for your unique situation.

Do you have the money to keep going? Financial considerations are a hard, cold, and very real part of this issue. Often the resurrection attempt involves paying for the body to be housed somewhere. If you have to borrow the money, how long will it take you to recover financially if the attempt fails? I don't recommend you gamble on "if it works then I will be fine." The truth is it might not work, and wisdom makes a plan based on the worst scenario, not the best one. If you blow through money in a few weeks that will take you a decade to recover from (depending on your financial situation), that may be a poor decision. Your attempt to walk in faith will put you under financial bondage. On the other hand, God may lead you to do exactly that and then provide the means for you to come out from the bondage to debt, with a resurrected loved one to boot! God is not limited by money troubles, so you don't have to be either, but this is still a very real consideration, and there is no shame in deciding it is simply something you cannot manage. Again, this is a situational thing you will have to decide (and live with the decision). Wise counsel is recommended.

Another question to consider is are you actually standing in faith, or has this moved into denial? It is legitimately possible to couch denial in "faith" terms. In other words, you may have shifted away from believing the person is going to return, but you are having trouble coping with the loss and don't want to deal with it. The longer you try to raise him, the longer you can push the unpleasant grief away. This is unwise and is probably a good reason *to* stop—at least for a season. Under such circumstances, the attempt has probably gone on for weeks already, not just a few hours or days, and you may need to work on finding a way to move on. I don't say this to suggest that grief means you need to stop, but if it has become unhealthy, it may be time to go forward with your life.

Is the body even still there? If the body has been buried, I personally recommend you stop. This sounds like a strange piece of advice, but I know of multiple situations where people are trying to raise their beloved years and years after the fact. It can get to the point where it becomes an unhealthy obsession, completely halts the grieving process, and is essentially detrimental not just to you but to those around you. When you are emotionally paralyzed to the point where you cannot get past the fact that the person is dead and the attempt failed so you keep trying, you are most likely being bound by demons who intend to keep you in denial and/or grief, and this doesn't bode well for your future. In this case it shortchanges your own life because you are so focused on trying to continually bring the person back that you don't live an abundant life of your own. I am not saying this applies if it is hours or days after the fact, but if you are months or years later still trying to raise someone and it is sucking the life out of you, this is a good indicator that you need to get help to move on.

Practically speaking, if the body is buried underground, for the resurrection to succeed the body will have to be both supernaturally translocated to an aboveground location and simultaneously resurrected. We don't typically have crypts or tombs that someone can climb their way out of if he returns—he will have to break out of a coffin in a sealed vault beneath a layer of dirt in the middle of an otherwise uninhabited field. And while God is the God of the impossible and *can* do anything, there comes a point where you do have to move forward on some level. I am probably the first to suggest resurrection any and every time, but you have to use wisdom and learn to recognize when enough is enough. I suggest that unless God has clearly spoken otherwise, when you decide to bury is a good time to stop attempting a resurrection. If it is someone else's decision to bury and you are praying from the sidelines so to speak, then I recommend stopping once the body is buried as well although it seems entirely reasonable to me to pray up until the minute the body is in the ground and being covered over.

If you or those around you are able to get clear guidance from God, ask Him to show you what to do, and if it comes to that point (which hopefully it will not), to lead you in when to stop. Two different women I spoke with who prayed for their deceased loved ones, the Lord gave specific dates by which the family member would either be raised or the family should stop praying. When those dates came, even though it hurt their hearts, they stopped praying according to the Lord's direction. If you don't know how to hear from God, then look at the situation with the recommendations and questions shared above and make your best decision possible. At the end of the day you can't really make the "wrong" decision if you do your best. God is very kind and will generally let you know one way or another what to do.

With all of that said, let me contradict myself here with the following: God is always about life. He has never given up on us and is not threatened by death. The Bible suggests that eventually everyone will be raised up at some point anyway (1 Thessalonians 4:16-17)—so literally zero people will stay dead long-term. God doesn't have a limited window of time when He is willing to let someone come back and if you are outside of that time window then you are stuck. No, literally at any moment you could get your loved one back—even if it is a decade after the fact. Deciding when to stop trying to resurrect is in some ways the difference between what I will call the "active phase" and "passive phase." An active phase is the period of intentional resurrection that has been discussed in this book. The passive phase is where you are generally believing he or she will return, but are not acting on it. You hold out hope in your heart, but there is no significant action and possibly no prayer toward that end. This can go on for years—decades even. On the one hand there is nothing wrong with this; on the other, it can be extremely unhealthy as mentioned before, entirely depending on one's approach. This is yet again situational, and wise council is again recommended.

I should also mention that if you are in an unsafe situation—where it is physically not safe to stay with a dead body and trying to resurrect him is putting your own life in danger, that is foolish and you should stop immediately unless God is clearly showing you otherwise. This would likely be very uncommon, but I feel it important to say. Prioritize keeping your life over that of the deceased—get yourself to safety and work out the rest of the details later. The body cannot get any more dead than it already is, and adding your death to the situation will not help anyone. Get safe first, then work out the resurrection details.

Finally, I want to express my heart on this: When I say it is time to move on, that doesn't mean you can't ever pray for your loved one again or hold out faith in your heart that someday he or she will return. It just can't rule your life as I have seen it do with some. Like I have said before, God's will as revealed in the Bible is for death to never occur, and for us to destroy it and resurrect the person every time it does occur. The reality is that sometimes the resurrection doesn't happen, and when it doesn't, we have to figure out how to move forward with our lives anyway. It's an unfortunate part of this business, but it comes with the territory. Again, men and women of God have resurrected people who have been dead for years and years, so time is not a limiting factor to God; it can be for us, and that is why the idea of stopping is so situational and can only be decided on an individual basis. With that in mind, the next section is geared toward looking at what we do if the deceased doesn't return and we have stopped trying to raise them.

CHAPTER 6

THE PRICE OF FAILURE

Resurrection attempts currently fail more often than they succeed, and unfortunately, those who fail usually pay a price. This can come in a variety of ways, but it's there somewhere. Someone once said that faith is spelled "R-I-S-K" and risk doesn't always pan out in your favor. On the other hand, those who never try to resurrect pay a different price, which is hopelessness and a near-guarantee they will never have their loved one back again this side of heaven.

A failed resurrection doesn't mean God is not faithful, God doesn't love you, God doesn't care, etc. A failed resurrection means that possibly hundreds of things took place behind the scenes that we simply don't know about—witchcraft, word curses, lack of faith, demonic resistance, the deceased person choosing not to return to earth, and other things we simply don't even know exist that still cause problems. It is advised to not change your beliefs about God and His love and goodness based on the results of a failed resurrection.

I should clarify something here before moving on—there are two ways to look at failure. The first is that failure means you didn't successfully raise the person, and that is how I use the term here. The second is that you didn't even *try* to raise them. On some level, God has told all of us to raise the dead, but at the end of the day, we really can only pray for the dead and they will either return or not. I believe that one version of failure is to not step out and try. If you have been obedient to God and made an honest attempt to try to resurrect someone, you are a success in God's eyes regardless of the results, and you can feel proud that you tried when many are not willing to do so. So while I refer to failure here in general as the dead person not returning to life, you are not a failure if it doesn't work.

Nevertheless, picking up the pieces of a failed attempt can in some ways be more difficult than if one had never made an effort in the first place. People can lose friends when they decide to stand in faith on God's promise of resurrection. While it seems like a stupid reason, it happens. The fact is that if the resurrection worked, the ex-friends probably wouldn't have responded the same way, and that's tough to deal with.

If you are a parent and your spouse is the one who died, you have kids you have to tend to during this process. Those children will not only have needed you during the attempt, but they will need you even more afterwards. Pay attention to the people who are important to you during the resurrection process—they are the ones who will often be supporting you and needing your support after the fact if things don't pan out.

One downside of failure is that the hope of return delays the grieving process. This can be especially hard if a child or spouse is the one who dies. The entire family will need to take time to grieve after the failed attempt as you may not have been able to before. This is important—don't skip this step. Even though a broken heart and delayed grieving was inevitable, I suggest that for those who had faith to begin with, the same God of Resurrection is also God the Healer, and He will gladly mend your broken heart. Continue to turn toward Him and seek His love even if the attempt fails because that is the time you will need Him all the more. While it is easy to read that and it may sound like a trite, pithy, religious saying, it isn't meant that way. God is truly the only real solution to heal inner pain.

With that said, it is important to allow time for the grieving process. Talk to friends and family, even see a counselor if that would help you. Dealing with grief doesn't mean you don't believe your loved one is in heaven—it means you are a human whose heart is hurting because someone you love died. That's normal and you are awesome. I am sorry for your loss and I pray God's grace touches you even now.

Chapter 7

Final Thoughts

Whether an individual resurrection attempt succeeds or fails, there is something we are all fighting for—the abundant life of Jesus Christ to be put on display before the many peoples of the earth. The Church—or at least the Western Church, is in a fairly poor state of health when it comes to this revelation, and as a result, resurrection from the dead has been a weak point in our current day. We may be good at many other aspects of Christian life, but this is an area for much learning and growth.

With that said, you and I are both pushing for the same thing—to see the dead raised. Whether one person's family member returns or not matters, and it matters a great deal, but at the same time we cannot let either failure or success turn us away from continuing to pursue the manifestation of this abundant life. Each time we pray, we sow our faith and it will never return to us without effect. There is no such thing as "crop failure" when we plant spiritual seeds. Galatians 6:7 says, "Do not be deceived: God cannot be mocked. A man reaps what he sows." It makes a mockery of God to think that we can pray for the dead to be raised and have it not eventually happen.

And while one failed attempt is still a loss for that dead person and their living loved ones, it is a step forward for us all. I believe there is a tipping point in the spirit—a point where we will reap a great harvest of the seeds of resurrection we have sown in prayer, and I believe that when that happens, we will see breakthrough in resurrection on an unprecedented level worldwide. Revelation 8 gives imagery of our prayers as incense before the throne, and it is combined with the fire from the altar in heaven (which is Jesus' sacrifice) and cast back down into the earth—a picture of our prayers being answered.

God is far more interested in raising the dead than we are. He hates death and the destruction and pain it brings to our lives, which is why in Revelation He promises us a day when we will eventually not cry anymore because the enemy Death has been defeated and all things will have been made new. Let us continue to pray and pursue this resurrection-breakthrough so that each and every time we set out to pray, the dead are raised.

THANK YOU FOR PURCHASING THIS BOOK

Thank you for reading *Practical Keys to Raise The Dead*. This book is designed to be a reference tool for anyone who is actively working to raise the dead. It is my hope and desire that this book will help activate people into seeing the dead raised. If you know anyone else who has a passion to see the resurrection life of Jesus Christ manifest in power, please consider sharing this book with them.

If you enjoyed this material, you can find more free content at www.thekingsofeden.com. Please consider leaving a review on Amazon.com so others can find this book more easily.

Other titles by Michael King:

God Signs Series:

Gemstones From Heaven

Feathers From Heaven

Non-series Books:

The Gamer's Guide to the Kingdom of God

ABOUT THE AUTHOR

Michael King is a prolific writer by day and a Registered Nurse by night. He hungrily explores all things spiritual and his love for God has given him a passion for signs, wonders, and miracles. Michael is married to a beautiful wife who doubles as his professional editor. He is known by family and friends for his proficiency in the prophetic and in healing prayer and energy work. His blog, TheKingsofEden.com, focuses on spirituality with a hint of health-related topics along with a dash of his fiction and fantasy writing. He is available for speaking engagements on request.